HOW TO BE AN
ANCIENT GREEK
ATHLETE

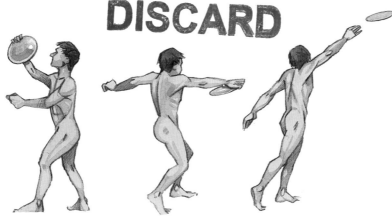

Written by
Jacqueline Morley

Illustrated by
David Antram

NATIONAL GEOGRAPHIC

Washington, D.C.

© The Salariya Book Company Ltd MMIV
Please visit the Salariya Book Company at:
www.salariya.com

First paperback printing 2008
First published in North America in 2005 by
NATIONAL GEOGRAPHIC SOCIETY
1145 17th Street, N.W.
Washington, D.C. 20036-4688

Paperback ISBN: 978-1-4263-0278-7

Library of Congress Cataloging-in-Publication Data available on request.

Printed in China

Series created and designed by David Salariya
Michael Ford, Editor

For tbe National Geographic Society
Bea Jackson, Art Director
Priyanka Lamichhane, Assistant Editor

Dr. Stephen Instone, Fact Consultant
Department of Greek and Latin, University College London

Photographic credits
t=top b=bottom c=center l=left r=right

The Ancient Art & Architecture Collection: 15
The Art Archive / Goulandris Foundation Athens /
Dagli Orti: 23
The Art Archive / Museo Nazionale Terme Rome /
Dagli Orti: 13
The Art Archive / Kanellopoulos Museum Athens /
Dagli Orti: 29
The Art Archive / Archaeological Museum Delphi /

Dagli Orti: 18
© Copyright The Trustees of The British Museum: 20
Shefton Museum, University of Newcastle-upon-Tyne:
11b
Every effort has been made to trace copyright holders.
The Salariya Book Company apologizes for any
unintentional omissions and would be pleased, in such
cases, to add an acknowledgment in future editions.

One of the world's largest nonprofit scientific and educational organizations, the National Geographic Society was founded
in 1888 "for the increase and diffusion of geographic knowledge." Fulfilling this mission, the Society educates and inspires
millions every day through its magazines, books, television programs, videos, maps and atlases, research grants, the National
Geographic Bee, teacher workshops, and innovative classroom materials. The Society is supported through membership dues,
charitable gifts, and income from the sale of its educational products. This support is vital to National Geographic's mission to
increase global understanding and promote conservation of our planet through exploration, research, and education.

For more information, please call 1-800-NGS LINE (647-5463) or write to the following address:
National Geographic Society
1145 17th Street N.W.
Washington, D.C. 20036-4688 U.S.A.
Visit us on the Web at **www.nationalgeographic.com/books**

Athletes Needed

Good at games? Eager to compete? Got what it takes to be a winner?

If that sounds like you, the city-state of Athens would like to hear from you. Athens is looking for strong, active young people to train in a variety of sports, and to compete in the city's famous Panathenaic games.

Applicants must be:

- of freeborn parentage—slaves cannot apply

- obedient to their trainers in all matters and to the rules of their chosen sport (fouls are punishable by whipping)

- aware that ancient Greek sports festivals are sacred events and that the reason for competing is to honor the gods

Job prospects are excellent. If you do well in the Athenian games you could be chosen to represent Athens at the great games at Olympia and win an Olympic crown.

Apply in person at your local gymnasion.

Contents

What You Should Know

Be prepared to travel back in time to around 450 B.C., your destination—ancient Greece. This is not one country like modern Greece; it is made up of many small states, each centered on a city or town, all fiercely independent and often at war with each other. Each state needs tough menfolk to defend it. That is why athletics is so important. Almost every city has its own games, held in honor of its protector god, and training for them keeps young people fit. The games at Athens, the most powerful city, are a very big affair. Winning there is a step on the way to the biggest win of all—victory at Olympia.

These games are open to men and boys only. There are festivals for women athletes as well, although they attract much less attention than the men's competitions. Girls, please apply separately for your special events.

Ancient Greece
c.450 B.C.

THRACE

Area in red shows the Greek world

AEGEAN SEA

Delphi

Athens

GREECE

ASIA MINOR

Olympia

Greek Islands

Sparta

MEDITERRANEAN SEA

CRETE

At the Gymnasion

You have an opportunity to apply for a job in a historic time and place. Athens in the fifth century B.C. is buzzing with new ideas. Its art will inspire people for thousands of years, and it has just established the first democracy. You'll be training at a gymnasion, which is like a school, a university, and a sports center all in one. Boys come for lessons and games; grown men come to train or watch the practice, and to argue about life and truth.

Athenians think the mind needs to be fed and strengthened, just like the body. Lessons include recitation, music, and singing. Older pupils also study philosophy and do archery and infantry drill.

You'll start training in a special place at the gymnasion called a palaestra, where you have lessons as well as athletic training.

What do we mean by democracy?

A music lesson at the gymnasion

Philosophy

At the gymnasion you'll find people listening to talkers known as "philosophers." These are thinkers of a new, particularly Athenian kind. They're seeking answers to life's big questions—the nature of the universe; the best way for people to be governed; the right way to live a good life.

▼ A lecture in one of the palaestra's study rooms. All rooms open onto a colonnade that surrounds a large central courtyard, used for boxing and wrestling. There are rooms for undressing (male athletes perform in the nude), for washing, and for storing equipment.

A teacher reciting poetry

A pupil

That everyone can vote—except women and slaves of course!

▲ This young man, about to become a citizen, is taking a compulsary two-year course on his city's traditions.

Greek literature

▶ As part of your training, you'll hear poetry and drama that's among the world's all-time best.

AZENE
RAMAH4II-II
IQEAOC<-NL
IOMGIAEVEON
RANORAONPEA
LEONE& A AOT

A fragment by the great female poet Sappho

Girls' education

◀ Girls and boys don't train together. That's frowned on in Athens, though it's normal in the state of Sparta. Disapproving Athenians call Spartan girls "thigh flashers." In Athens girls study at home, learning womanly skills, and train at women's palaestras, often attached to a temple of Artemis, goddess of hunting.

7

Sports and Recreation

The Greeks place a great deal of importance on physical exercise. As well as athletics at school, young boys play a number of games outside the gymnasion. Although they are only games, they will help sharpen your competitive edge and keep you fit.

Hockey

▶ A fast and furious type of hockey is played in pairs. Players "face off" and, using a curved stick, aim to push the ball or disc over their opponents' line.

That's it! You're over the back line.

Ball skills

▼ A boy balances a ball made from a pig's bladder on his thigh without touching it. He keeps the ball in the air by bouncing it back and forth from one knee to the other.

Team games

▲ Boys play *episkyros*, a game for two teams of equal numbers. A line is drawn between them and another behind each team. A ball is placed on the central line. Each team tries to throw the ball past the other, who must try to stop it and throw it back again. The winning team is the one who manages to get the ball past the other team and drive their opposition over the back line.

▲ Another favorite Greek game is called *ephedrismos* in which a *dioros* (stone) is set up at a distance and two players compete to knock it over by throwing balls. The loser has to give the winner a piggy-back ride and then try to find the *dioros*, with his "rider" covering his eyes.

Acrobatics

▶ Acrobatics are popular. Acrobats are used as children's entertainers. In this acrobatic stunt a man vaults onto the back of a horse from a takeoff ramp.

9

Go the Distance

If you're applying to be a runner you'll train right next to the palaestra in first-class facilities. There is an open air track and a covered one for practice in bad weather, each a *stadion* long (about 650 feet [200 m]). In the games there are a stadion and a double stadion race for sprinters. The starting line and the finish line are marked across the sand track by an inset band of stones.

A student being whipped for fouling

Age groups

For lessons and for training, pupils are divided according to age. The city's festival of games has similar categories. There are events for boys, for "beardless youths" (late teens), and for adults.

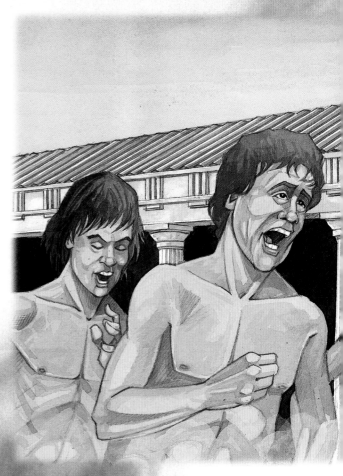

Obey the rules!

◄ Whatever your age you have to put up with strict discipline at all times. The head of the gymnasion (called the *gymnasiarchos*) is a stern person who decides the school's curriculum and appoints the teachers and coaches. He makes sure that his staff punish bad work and fouls with lashes from the long willow canes they all carry.

▼ These older boys are practicing for the gymnasion's annual competitions that assess pupils' progress.

Just two stadia to go.

Keeping clean

▲ Since you always exercise naked you won't have to worry about getting the right clothes for the job. The basic equipment for all athletes is a round flask of olive oil with a cord for hanging it on a peg, a sponge for washing yourself down, and a tool called a strigil. You warm up by rubbing yourself all over with the oil; the strigil is used for scraping it off when you've finished for the day. Then you shower in the palaestra washroom, where lion-headed spouts along the wall pour water into a series of tubs.

▲ A bronze strigil. Its curved blade is hollowed to collect the mixture of oil, sweat, and dust you'll be covered in.

Tests of Strength

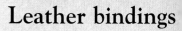

Boxing and wrestling are the palaestra's chief activities. You'll have to be tough to compete, for there aren't many safety rules. In boxing, the chief tactic is aiming blows at your opponent's head. There are no rounds and no time limit. You keep boxing until someone drops, and people can get killed. Even so there are boxing competitions for very young boys.

Wrestling is a test of strength and ruthlessness. There are two forms of the sport. In normal wrestling the object is to throw your opponent to the floor. The second form, pancration, is a violent type of wrestling that continues on the ground after a contestant has been thrown.

Anything goes

▶ In pancration wrestling almost anything goes—limb twisting, finger breaking, punching, jumping on your opponent, and strangulation. Only biting and gouging out eyes are not allowed. Younger boys are not expected to compete in pancration wrestling.

Leather bindings

◀ There are no boxing gloves. Instead the hands and wrists are bound with strips of leather up to 13 feet (4 m) long. These help to strengthen the wrists and protect the knuckles.

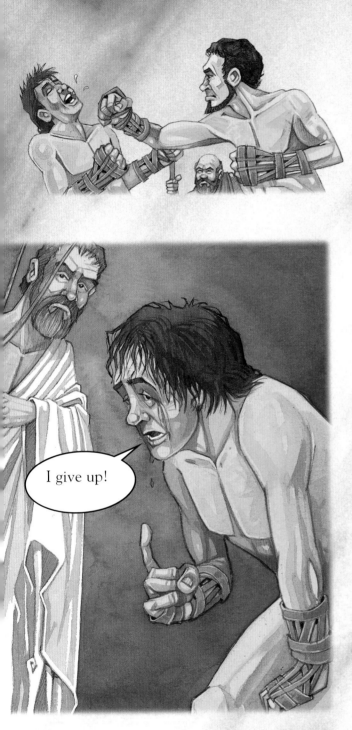

Hard lessons

◀ A new type of binding is gaining favor: a piece of fleece-lined leather bound around the forearm, wrists, and knuckles. A hard knuckle guard of laminated metal strips gives added protection and increases the harm done to an opponent. The leather bindings are nicknamed "ants," because they sting an opponent's skin and leave little nicks and grazes. The leather used is usually oxhide. Pigskin strips are banned because they make particularly painful wounds that are very slow to heal.

◀ The referee watches with his willow cane ready. Fouls are punishable by whipping. You can raise a finger to signal that you're ready to give up.

Broken nose

Bruised and battered

▶ This bronze statue of a boxer shows the wear and tear you can expect. He has a broken nose and blood (inlaid in copper) drips from his forehead, nose, cheek, and ear.

The Pentathlon

Beyond the running track is the practice area for javelin and discus throwing, and for the long jump. This is where you train if you want to compete in the pentathlon, which is made up of five events: sprinting, wrestling, jumping, discus throwing, and javelin throwing. It's a tough contest. Unless you have staying power, don't enter this contest.

The long jump

▼ The long jump is performed to the accompaniment of flute music. Rhythm is crucial to getting the right movement, and the music helps the athlete to establish the right rhythm. He grasps a weight in each hand and these help to carry him forward.

Discus tips

With his weight on his right foot and ▶ leaning slightly back, the discus thrower steadies the discus at shoulder height. He raises his arm and, as he starts his throw, bends and spins around to propel the discus.

First, grip the javelin with your right hand.

▲ Stretching his arms out in front of him, the athlete stands poised for a moment, listening to the flute player.

Jumping tips

◀ He rocks to and fro, breaks into a run, and as he leaps, swings the weights up in front of him. Once in the air they continue to pull him forward. As he descends he stretches his arms and legs forward and then swings the weights behind for added thrust.

Javelin tips

▼ Javelin throwers wrap a thin leather thong around the javelin shaft, making it end in a loop. This acts as a sling to help propel the javelin. The thong unwinds in flight.

▲ As he runs forward, the javelin thrower holds the tip of the javelin with his left hand to press it back against the loop. He releases the tip as he brings his right arm forward, slipping his fingers from the loop as he hurls the javelin. Learning to bind the javelin well is the secret of success.

Discus

Jumping weight

Javelin

Pick

► This ancient Greek vase painting commemorates the pentathlon. It shows a discus thrower and a javelin thrower taking their starting positions. A pair of weights for the long jump hangs behind them. The pick was used for digging the pit for the jumpers' soft landing.

15

Competing in the City Games

Each year you'll have a chance, if you are good enough, to compete in the annual Panathenaia, Athens's city games. Every fourth year the city hosts a much larger festival, the greater Panathenaic games, open to athletes throughout Greece, with big prizes to be won. Events include athletics, horse and chariot racing, and contests for kithara playing, flute playing, and accompanied singing.

Starting line with grooves

▲ This is your starting position: left foot forward, knees slightly bent, and arms outstretched. Your toes must be positioned in the two grooves cut in the band of stone that marks the starting line.

On your mark . . .

▼ The most important event is the stadion race. Its winner will be the hero of the games. If you do well in your training period you could be in one of these competitions.

Get set . . .

▲ Runners take up their positions behind a starting barrier formed of two cords stretched across the track, one at knee height and one at waist height. The cords are stretched between two posts, which are kept in an upright position by the starter. He stands well back, holding a cord that will spring the posts forward when it is released.

Go!

▲ The starter cries "Apite!" (go) as he releases the cord that catapults the starting gate to the ground. You're off—good luck!

Longer distances

▶ Athletic events are held in the agora, the big open marketplace. A running track is marked with lanes, each with a post at the far end to show runners in the double stadion where they must turn. A separate post marks the turning point for long-distance runners.

Turning post

Prizes

There are prizes for first, second, and third place (and sometimes for fourth and fifth place, too). Some are paid in money; some, in olive oil in costly jars with an image of Athena on the side. The winner of the boys' stadion gets 50 jars, each holding nearly ten and a half gallons (40 l) of oil (a total value of about $11,000).

Athena

▶ Athena, protectress of Athens, watches over the games. A giant statue of her stands in her temple overlooking the city. You must always remember you are competing in honor of the goddess.

17

At the Hippodrome

After your race you can relax and enjoy the other events. The horse races are always exciting. Because they need a long track they are run outside the city on a course known as a hippodrome.

Danger!

▼ The four-horse chariot race is run over 12 laps of the hippodrome. There is a turning post but no barrier in the center of the track. There have been some nasty head-on crashes.

Glory

◄ A winner often has a monument made to celebrate his triumph. This bronze charioteer commemorates a victory in a four-horse chariot race of 474 B.C.

Faster! Faster!

Stepped starting positions

Starting blocks

▲ The horses start from a V-shaped series of stalls, closed by cords. The cords of the two outer stalls are dropped and their horses take off. They trigger the cords of the next stalls as they pass, and so on, until all the horses are running abreast.

The winners

Chariot racing calls for split-second handling of the horses, especially at the turns, and successful teams are famous. Yet it is the owner of the horses who wins, not the charioteer, who is usually a slave or a professional driver. A woman can win a prize at the all-male games if she owns a winning team. Owning and training horses is expensive, so you have to be very rich to compete in these events.

▶ There is also a two-horse chariot race. For both races the chariot is a light vehicle with a metal or wicker cage around the driver's stand.

Keeping Fit to Fight

Watching the adult events you'll notice that many involve fighting skills. Although the main purpose of the festival is religious, Athens wants all its young men to be able to defend it and sees the games as a great boost to military training.

War practice

Contests with a military slant include javelin throwing from horseback to hit a target and cavalry charges by opposing teams.

Bronze figure of a woman athlete running

▲ Men and women don't mix publicly in ancient Athens, so girls take it for granted that they must have separate games.

Women's athletics

◄ Every four years women have their own festival in honor of the goddess Hera; it is held at Olympia like the top all-male games. Although Athens sends a team, women's sports are given much less importance here than in Sparta, which prides itself on training all its young people to be tough.

Phyrric dance

◀ These dancers, bearing shields, are from a marble relief celebrating their victory in the phyrric dancing contest. This is a sort of military ballet in which competing teams perform movements based on the various skills a fighter needs in attack and defense. The aim of this event is to promote military precision and teamwork.

Torch race

▼ The torch relay race is a high point in the festival. Starting from the famous Academy gymnasion outside the city, ten teams compete to pass a flaming torch from runner to runner through the streets of Athens to the heights of the Acropolis. The winning team is the first to reach Athena's altar with a burning torch and light the fire for the chief sacrifices of her festival.

Hoplitodromoi
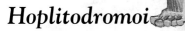

▲ Runners known as *hoplitodromoi* (runners in armor) take part in a race wearing helmets and carrying heavy shields. Although this race is run over the same length as the double stadion race, it calls for different skills, needing special strength as well as speed. Rarely does the same athlete win both events.

At Elis

▼ For ten months before the games the judges are housed in a special building at Elis, to be trained in Olympic regulations and rules of the various events.

Palaestra

Theater

Agora

Temple

Judges' lodging

Good athletes are ambitious, so you'll certainly be aiming to represent Athens at one of the big interstate games. Four cities host these, in a four-year cycle—Isthmia and Nemea twice every four years, and Delphi and Olympia once. If you're chosen for Olympia, the top competition, you'll join other contenders at the little city of Elis, which organizes the games. The 50-member Olympic council is based at Elis. Every four years this small city-state is turned into an athletic training town (the equivalent of the modern Olympic village).

Gathering crowds

Athletes bring their trainers and often family and friends as well. Tourists and fans come to watch them, and Elis is soon crowded with people.

Some athletes favor special diets, gorging themselves on cheese or meat.

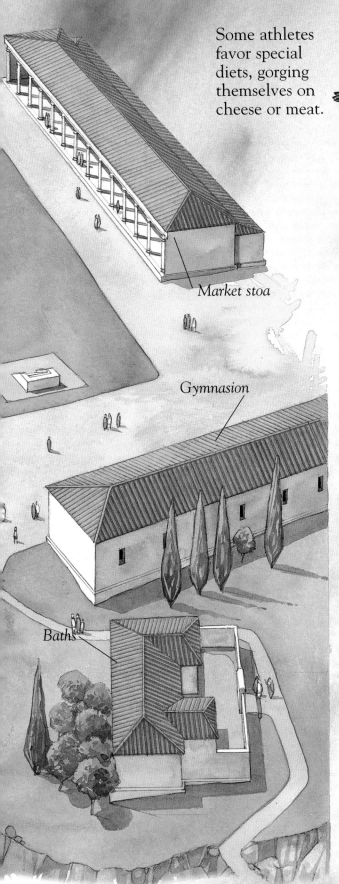

Market stoa

Gymnasion

Baths

An athlete arriving at the games, fit and confident

Competitors must reach Elis a month before the games start to receive final training from the ten judges who umpire its events. Athletes arriving late are fined, and any who do not pay are flogged.

Olympic truce

▼ A month before the games, heralds are sent to every part of Greece to announce the sacred Olympic truce. During this time all war must cease to allow safe travel to the games.

Arriving at Olympia

The day before the games a procession of judges, athletes, trainers, families, friends, and onlookers begins the long march to Olympia, where crowds of spectators are waiting to welcome them. Before entering the site, the judges must purify themselves. They wash in a sacred spring and are sprinkled with pig's blood.

Zeus

◄ A giant statue of Zeus, king of the gods, dominates his temple at the heart of Olympia. It was built by the famous sculptor Phidias. The games are held in honor of Zeus. Every winning athlete adds to that honor through the excellence he has achieved.

Nymphaeum (fountain)

Feasting hall for victors

Temple of Hera

Gymnasion

Altar of Zeus

Altis (sacred grove)

Palaestra

Swimming pool

Workshop of Phidias

Lodging for official guests

Baths

Registering for the games

▼ Before the start all athletes go to the *bouleterion* (council chamber). There, the judges demand proof of age and assess how close physically each is to adulthood in order to assign them to the men's or boys' events.

In the *bouleterion*, athletes and trainers make a vow before the statue of Zeus Horkios (Zeus of the oath), that they will do nothing dishonest in the games.

Preparing the running track

▲ Lots of preparation has gone on. Tracks have been dug, sprinkled with water, and rolled smooth. Lanes have been marked with white earth.

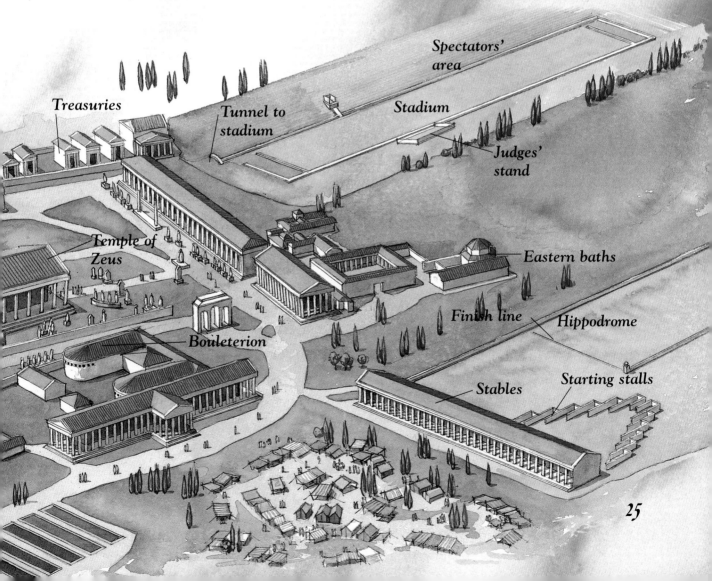

Treasuries

Tunnel to stadium

Spectators' area

Stadium

Judges' stand

Temple of Zeus

Eastern baths

Bouleterion

Finish line

Hippodrome

Stables

Starting stalls

25

The *Panselinos*

The date of the festival is always fixed to ensure that the opening events (horse races and pentathlon) will be followed by a night of the full moon. Since the new day in ancient Greece begins at dusk, the full moon (*panselinos*) heralds the religious high point of the games, the day of the great sacrifice at the altar of Zeus.

The altar of Zeus

▼ On the day of the *panselinos* priests and judges lead a procession to Zeus's altar, a mound formed by the accumulated ashes of past sacrifices.

Sacrifice and feasting

▼ Athletes and ambassadors from the various city-states follow behind with offerings, including a hundred oxen given by the people of Elis.

The oxen are slaughtered at the altar and their thighs burned on the altar-top as an offering to Zeus. The rest of the meat is roasted for the crowd.

▼ After the sacrifice the crowd joins in a general feasting. Smoke is thick from the fires. People are cooking delicacies to add to those generous handouts of sacrifical meat.

Roughing it

Spectators have created a tent city around the sacred grove. It's cramped and uncomfortable, especially if it rains, but no one minds. It's noisy too. There are peddlers and fortune-tellers shouting; magicians doing tricks; philosophers arguing; poets reciting and applauding each other; and painters and sculptors, hoping for a commission from some winning athlete, setting out their wares.

The Olympic Crown

At Olympia you need to win. There are no prizes for runners-up. Top honors go to the stadion winner; the year's games are named after him. Ancient Greek historians dated events by saying whose Olympiad they occurred in. So, if you want your name recorded in history, you must win the stadion race.

Judges' enclosure

▼ The judges watch from a stand near the finish line. Each winner will be showered with ribbons and flowers by his cheering fans.

An enthusiastic crowd

▲On the last day of events the grassy banks around the stadium are packed with spectators for the footraces. The athletes get ready in a room just outside the stadium and come onto the track through a tunnel under the bank. The runners in each event wait tensely in the tunnel for their race to be called.

▼ As each athlete steps from the dark tunnel onto the track, his name and city are announced by a herald. The crowd cheers or boos as each runner appears.

Nikodemos of Athens!

Singing praises

◄ Great Olympic deeds are celebrated in a special kind of poem called a victory ode. Winning athletes, or their admirers, often commission a famous poet to write an ode and recite it publicly.

A symbolic prize

▼ You don't compete at Olympia for the sake of a valuable prize. Every victor has the same reward, a crown of olive leaves cut with a golden sickle from the trees in Olympia's sacred grove. The vase painting below shows a winged figure, representing victory, giving a winner the most coveted prize in ancient Greek sport, an Olympic crown.

Crown of olive leaves

Nike, Greek goddess of victory

Your interview

Answer these questions to test your knowledge about being a Greek athlete, then look at page 32 to find out if you have what it takes to get the job.

Q1 In ancient Greece, where is educating girls and boys together considered normal?
A in Sparta
B in Athens
C in Elis

Q2 What does the full moon (*panselinos*) herald at the Olympic Games?
A the crowning of Nike, goddess of victory
B the purification of the judges with pig's blood
C the sacrifice at the altar of Zeus

Q3 What are the chief activities in the palaestra?
A the long jump and sprinting
B boxing and wrestling
C hockey and piggy-back riding

Q4 Which of the following are included in the five events of the pentathlon?
A discus and javelin throwing
B boxing and hockey
C *episkyros* and *ephedrismos*

Q5 In whose honor are the Olympic Games held?
A the god Zeus
B the goddess Nike
C the goddess Athena

Q6 Where are chariot races held?
A at the gymnasion
B at the colonnade
C at the hippodrome

Q7 Who are the *hoplitodromoi*?
A wrestlers
B racers
C judges

Q8 What does a winner of the Olympic Games receive?
A a crown of olive leaves
B a golden crown
C a jar of olive oil

Glossary

Academy. A famous school of philosophy near the city of Athens.

Agora. An open marketplace.

Bouleterion. A council chamber.

Bronze. A brown-colored metal made by melting together copper and tin.

Cavalry. Soldiers who fight on horse-back.

Citizen. In ancient Greece this meant an inhabitant of a city-state who had the right to decide how it was governed. Tradespeople, women, and slaves did not have this right.

Colonnade. A walkway, open along one side, with columns on the other side supporting the roof.

Curriculum. The course of studies taught in a place of learning.

Democracy. The system of government in ancient Athens, where every citizen could vote on how the city was run.

Discus. A large, flat, circular weight, usually made of bronze.

Gymnasion. A school for boys. The word literally means "place of naked people."

Herald. An official announcer.

Inlaid. Set into the surface of an object, such as a table, in a decorative design.

Kithara. A plucked string instrument, a large heavy form of the lyre.

Laminated. Beaten into a thin metal layer.

Olympiad. The four-year interval between Olympic games by which ancient Greeks measured time.

Olympic truce. A time when all war must cease to allow safe travel to the Olympic games.

Palaestra. An exercise ground.

Pancration. A violent form of wrestling that did not stop when one opponent was thrown to the floor.

Pentathlon. An athletic event consisting of five sports.

Relief. A sculpture carved so that shapes on the surface stand out from the background.

Sparta. The city-state that challenged Athens as the major power in ancient Greece.

Stadion. A measure of length, equal to 600 ancient feet (about 607 modern feet). Also the name of the race of that length (roughly equivalent to the present-day 200-yard [200-m] dash). Plural *stadia*.

Stoa. A covered colonnade.

Strigil. A tool for scraping the skin clean.

Thong. A narrow strip of leather, used like a lace or strap.

Wicker. A material woven from flexible canes.

Index

Page numbers in boldface refer to illustrations.

Further Reading

Oxlade, Chris and David Ballheimer. *Olympics* (Eyewitness Books). Dorling Kindersley, 2000.

Woff, Richard. *The Ancient Greek Olympics.* Oxford University Press, 2000.

Have You Got the Job?

Count up your correct answers (*below right*) and find out if you got the job.

Your score:

8 Congratulations! You deserve the Olympic crown.

7 Nearly there. Keep attending the city games.

5–6 Promising prospect. Try running with a helmet and shield to build up your muscles.

3–4 Best stick to the boys' games for now.

Fewer than 3 Why not try something less physical?

Q1 (A) page 7
Q2 (C) page 26
Q3 (B) pages 12–13
Q4 (A) pages 14–15
Q5 (A) page 24
Q6 (C) pages 18–19
Q7 (B) page 21
Q8 (A) page 29